Amazing Manifestation Strategies
— Book 3

THE MANIFESTATION MINDSET

How to Think Like a True Manifestor
and Overcome the Doubts Blocking Your
Success

FORBES ROBBINS BLAIR

Edit/Design by Rob Morrison

i

The Manifestation Mindset / Forbes Robbins Blair

DEDICATION

This book is dedicated to all the manifestors who are frustrated with their results. Here's my effort to help you become successful.

And not least of all, this is to my family, friends, clients and personal development writers who each help me find more dedication to this fascinating subject. Thank you.

CONTENTS

MANIFESTATION, MAGIC BEANS & TOUGH LOVE
.... 1

THE MENTAL LAW THAT CAN RUIN YOUR
SUCCESS—AND HOW TO OVERCOME IT 7

HOW I DEVELOPED THE MANIFESTATION
MINDSET, AND WHY YOU CAN DO IT FASTER 11

MANIFESTORS VERSUS DABBLERS 17

MINDSET STRATEGY 1: APPRECIATE YOUR
MANIFESTATION POWER 21

MINDSET STRATEGY 2: INCREASE AND
REINFORCE YOUR KNOWLEDGE 27

MINDSET STRATEGY 3: STIMULATE YOUR
CREATIVE, INTUITIVE MIND 33

MINDSET STRATEGY 4: CONDUCT
MANIFESTATION EXPERIMENTS 39

MINDSET STRATEGY 5: TRACK YOUR
MANIFESTATIONS 49

MINDSET STRATEGY 6: PERFORM ACTIVE AND
PASSIVE AFFIRMATIONS 55

MINDSET STRATEGY 7: SELF-GUIDED
MEDITATION FOR MANIFESTORS 61

"Manifestation Powerhouse Meditation" 65

MINDSET STRATEGY 8: WEAR A "MAGIC"
MANIFESTATION TALISMAN 69

MINDSET STRATEGY 9: BUILD POSITIVE
EXPECTATION 75

HOW TO KNOW WHEN YOU HAVE ACHIEVED
THE MANIFESTATION MINDSET 81

BOOKS+ 85

ABOUT THE AUTHOR 89

REQUEST 91

"All that we are is the result of what we have thought. It is founded on thought. It is based on thought."

—Buddha, *The Dhammapada*

MANIFESTATION, MAGIC BEANS & TOUGH LOVE

"Manifest millions right now!"

"Instantly attract everything you want in life without any effort!!"

"Since I did it, so can you."

"It's easy when you learn the secret that only I can tell you."

Sound familiar? These are often the claims of manifestation books and gurus. Well... if you believe that, there are some wondrous magic beans I'd like to sell to you. Just throw the beans out of your bedroom window and climb the giant beanstalk to the life of your dreams. And, make sure to tell the Golden Goose I sent you.

But enough is enough, seriously. You are smarter than that. You know that's all just hype. Now, don't get me wrong: manifesting can bring you what you want. However, it's time for a reality check about what manifestation really means. It's time for some tough love. But don't worry, it won't be all that tough.

The essential message of the manifestation principle is that your thoughts manifest your reality—whether

that reality is fortunate or unfortunate, pleasant or painful, extraordinary or common.

Seems simple enough, right? But mastery of this principle doesn't come easily. I've been actively working with manifestation since 1992, and my journey to mastery is far from complete. However, I have learned a lot over the years, and I would love to share what has worked for me and for many of my clients and readers.

I am familiar with many methods that can help people hone their manifestation power. But I have yet to find a method that always works for everyone. That's understandable because consciousness is fluid, and its changing tides can be tricky to navigate. Truly understanding manifestation is complex. Don't let anyone tell you differently.

The upside is that you can gain greater proficiency and accuracy at manifesting the things you want by acquiring what I call the Manifestation Mindset. The purpose of this book is to help you do just that.

If you believe you already have the right mindset, but you still struggle to manifest prosperity, healthy relationships or a satisfying work life, you just might want to reconsider your assumption. This book can help you pinpoint the source of the problem.

Why You Need This Book

I wrote this book because its message and strategies are essential to your success with manifestation. Let me explain why.

After the release of the first two books in the Amazing Manifestation Strategies series, I got quite a bit of feedback from readers who tried the techniques and strategies recommended in them. Some of my readers emailed to say "thank you" because they manifested new relationships, more money, and better jobs. Others were upset with the techniques because they still hadn't experienced the results they wanted.

This puzzled me. I wondered how some of my readers could practice the same manifestation techniques and get excellent results while other people could experience little or no results.

Are some people just better at manifesting than others, I wondered? Do those "successful manifestors" possess certain natural qualities anyone could duplicate?

Are unsuccessful manifestors engaging in negative thinking where their actions lead to failure? Can their problems be identified and stopped, or even prevented?

To help me understand this mystery, I exchanged emails with many people from both groups. I asked each person about their life, experiences, behaviors, beliefs and feelings about manifestation. I also asked them to explain what actions they took during their process.

After the emails poured in, some patterns quickly became clear. I found the difference between successful and unsuccessful manifestors could be summed in one word: *mindset*.

You may wonder what I mean by mindset. Here's a working definition:

Mindset refers to a disposition that predetermines how you interpret what happens, and how you respond to it.

Having a positive, stable and balanced manifestation mindset far exceeds the importance of any other technique because it is foundational. If you don't have it, even the wisdom from the best Law of Attraction teachers will fail.

The correct mindset allows legitimate manifestation techniques to work so beautifully you'll find good things will happen for you most of the time. When you have the right mindset, you will come to know you are the one who makes those good things happen.

It reminds me of a favorite scene from *The Matrix* movie, where the Oracle tells Neo: "I'm going to let you in on a little secret. Being the One is just like being in love. No one can tell you you're in love. You just know it, balls to bones."

And like the character Neo, you must know that your mind and body are at work manufacturing your reality at all times. This *knowingness and awareness* are at the heart of the Manifestation Mindset. This book shows you how to get them with easy, accessible strategies you can work with right now.

It is never too early or too late to develop this all-important mindset. If you are new to manifestation, you can use this book to train your mind for success from the beginning so you avoid the frustrations and the set-backs so common to many aspiring manifestors. If you are an experienced manifestor and are still unsatisfied with your results, you can begin today to end self-sabotage and start to allow yourself to reach a successful mindset for almost any goal.

Once you have improved your mindset, you will become aware that your manifestation power is always switched ON. You will understand that there is never a time when you are not in the manifesting process.

This new way of thinking will have a profound effect on all of your manifestation endeavors and any Law of Attraction technique you will ever use.

So whether you want more money, a passionate relationship, to change your career or anything else, you will have the inner resources to manifest what you desire.

THE MENTAL LAW THAT CAN RUIN YOUR SUCCESS—AND HOW TO OVERCOME IT

Perhaps the greatest benefit of attaining the manifestation mindset is it helps you to eradicate hidden doubts about manifestation power.

It's crucial to eliminate doubt because it can sabotage your manifesting efforts. It can trigger the mental law known as the *Law of Reversed Effect*. This law states that the harder you consciously try to do something, the more difficult it becomes. Here's an example: Remember when you took a school test and tried in vain to recall some fact you were sure you studied? The harder you tried to remember, the more anxious you became, the more the answer eluded you. Your subconscious did the reverse of what your conscious mind intended, and that's called the Law of Reversed Effect.

When you consciously try too hard to manifest something, your subconscious mind is resistant. The subconscious is the part which carries out your manifestation intentions. So you need to use your conscious mind in a relaxed and structured way to get the results you want. The more conscious force you apply, the more difficult it will be to succeed at manifesting.

7

The Law of Reversed Effect is subtle and tricky though, and explains why many people never get anywhere with manifestation techniques—especially when it comes to the things they most want. They hope that if they repeat more affirmations or visualize more clearly or for a longer period of time, the Universe will magically reward their sincere effort. But their excessive effort is an attempt to mask doubts about their manifestation power, so they unwittingly set up a conflict between their conscious and subconscious. And that conflict is the big block to their success.

I don't want that to happen to you. If it has already happened, I want to give you a way to overcome it.

The solution is to possess genuine confidence and effortless expectation. If the school test-taker has adequately studied and has enough subject knowledge, she can stop worrying about the test results. She can just summon the information without effort and with little doubt about the outcome. Manifesting works the same way.

When you know the power is real and at your command, you rise above the Law of Reversed Effect. Quiet confidence replaces any doubts about your power and the manifestation principle.

When the conscious self and your subconscious self are in harmony about what you want and your power to manifest it, this mindset radiates to the Universe and automatically attracts opportunities to confirm your mindpower.

This mindset will have an impact on everything you want to manifest. There will be times you won't have to employ any manifestation techniques at all. Instead, you will be able to *will* what you want because you know that your thoughts have pulling power.

HOW I DEVELOPED THE MANIFESTATION MINDSET, AND WHY YOU CAN DO IT FASTER

Now that you understand the importance and the benefits of the manifestation mindset, the question is how do you go about creating, establishing and developing it?

Let's be clear: It's not as simple as wanting or affirming it. For the kind of deep-seated confidence and awareness we're talking about, something more intense is required.

People with the manifestation mindset rarely acquire it on purpose, and they certainly don't do it overnight. At some point, they are exposed to the concepts of the Law of Attraction and Manifestation and that sends them on a long journey of knowledge-seeking, contemplation, introspection and experience.

Over time, their minds become trained to look at themselves and the world through the lens of manifestation. They develop and refine this lens by habitually thinking and doing specific things that affirm their mindset.

For instance, it took me many years to cultivate my current manifestation mindset. It's nothing I did on purpose. One thing just led to another.

I can trace the start of its formation to a single event. When I was twelve, my family took a vacation to the Grand Canyon in Arizona. It was fun and exciting alright. But I most clearly recall what happened while we drove across the desert back home to the east coast. As I casually looked through the window and up at the sky, I noticed a peculiar cloud formation. It looked like a closed hand except for the index finger pointing heavenward. And I'll never forget my father's response to me, "You were the one who spotted it, Forbes. So it must be a message for you."

I remember taking his words to heart at that time. And I deeply considered that God—as I understood the Divine then—was communicating with me. God's message seemed to be that I should pay attention to my connection with Him.

From that moment on, I looked for possible message signposts from God that might appear around me. That day, I became more spiritually aware which led me through many mansions and corridors of religious thought, philosophy and metaphysics.

Eventually I learned much about manifestation, which is not a religion at all, but it's a metaphysical principle that has become part of my way of thinking.

Manifestation informs me that everything in the Universe is made of thought-energy, and that the circumstances of life are controlled by it.

I have formulated some strategies about thought and energy that have helped me and my clients gain more conscious control over what we manifest. One of those strategies is to establish and reinforce the right mindset.

The good news is that you do not need to spend years to establish the manifestation mindset. *It will only take a tiny fraction of that time because you are choosing to develop it on purpose.* Because it is something you want to do, you can speed up the process tremendously by engaging in certain activities in a concentrated way. Those activities will help you to train your thought process and shift into a successful manifestor in just days.

How I Developed Mindset Strategies:
An Overview

I have identified nine attitudes and behaviors shared by many successful manifestors.

These characteristics are not the only ways manifestors think or behave; however, I believe the following characteristics contribute most to their positive mindsets and will help you as well. Successful manifestors:

* Acknowledge and express gratitude for what they have already manifested

* Constantly grow in knowledge about manifestation from many sources

* View manifestation as intuitive and creative rather than just mechanical

13

* Are confident in their overall ability to manifest based on their past successes

* Keep track of their manifestation results

* Use affirmations and guided meditation to assist their manifestation power

* Recognize manifesting as constant and ever-present in their lives

* Are persistent and expect to succeed

Based on these positive attributes and my knowledge and experience, I created nine mindset strategies for this book which will work together to help you establish the manifestation mindset in as little as 21 days. All of them are easy to do. Most can be performed quickly. Some of them you will do each day; others you will perform less often.

Here is an overview and introduction for each strategy:

* *Mindset Strategy 1: Appreciate Your Manifestation Power.* Take a minute or two each day to recognize your manifestation abilities at work in your "ordinary" life. This develops a habitual awareness that your power is already active, and is responsible for the good things you attract. I'll also share an efficient way to establish this habit.

* *Mindset Strategy 2: Increase and Reinforce Your Knowledge.* Fifteen minutes a day before bedtime, read material to learn and reinforce the principles

of manifestation and to support a belief in your ability to access your power. This is about more than mere information-gathering. It's about saturating your mind with the idea of manifestation, which will stimulate your power.

* *Mindset Strategy 3: Stimulate Your Intuitive, Creative Mind.* Two or three times a week, watch certain kinds of movies to connect with the creative part of your mind. This strategy helps you get beyond the illusion of limitations caused by the appearance of linear time and space. I list many examples of the types of movies that have worked well for me and my coaching clients.

* *Mindset Strategy 4: Conduct Manifestation Experiments.* At least once a week, test your manifestation powers with mini-manifestation experiments. This gives you the opportunity to observe the cause-effect relationship between your thoughts and manifestation. I reveal five mini-experiments you can use for this purpose.

* *Mindset Strategy 5: Track Your Manifestations.* Keep a daily record of your manifestation insights and observations. Productivity experts have proved that people who keep track of their progress tend to perform better. I'll show you some entries in my own journal to give you ideas about how to write yours.

* *Mindset Strategy 6: Perform Active and Passive Affirmations.* For a few minutes every day, recite or

listen to affirmations that support your manifestation power. This is a classic strategy, and it works. I also offer some original, potent affirmations you can use for this purpose.

* Mindset Strategy 7: Use Self-Guided Meditation. For 10-15 minutes three times a week, employ a guided meditation designed to stimulate your manifestation thinking and accelerate your powers. I provide a powerful one called "The Manifestation Powerhouse Meditation" you can use right away, and you don't even have to close your eyes!

* Mindset Strategy 8: Wear a "Magic" Manifestation Talisman. With this strategy, you carry an object that perpetually reminds you that your manifesting power is ready and available. While this is mostly a psychological device, there is also a thought-energy component that makes this strategy work like "magic." And I'll tell you all about that.

* Mindset Strategy 9: Build Positive Expectation. Ask yourself simple, specific questions throughout each day to create positive anticipation about the manifestation of your desires. Expectation not only helps develop your mindset, but it naturally leads to greater manifesting success.

MANIFESTORS VERSUS DABBLERS

According to Maxwell Maltz, author of the classic bestselling book *Psycho-Cybernetics*, it takes a minimum of 21 days to secure a new habit. And that's exactly what these strategies are meant to help you do:

The nine mindset strategies will lead you to form new habits of thinking, feeling and acting which will be in alignment with manifestation principles.

I do not mean you must wait three weeks to see some remarkable changes though. Within days of implementing these strategies, you will start to notice overwhelming evidence that your manifestation abilities are real and active.

However, what will take time is the lasting shift in your patterns, attitudes and ways of responding to life. For now, trust that these strategies will have a cumulative impact on your thinking habits. They will help to produce the most effective manifestation mindset.

Commit to this goal, and immerse yourself in these strategies for a minimum of 21 days. Then you may apply your

transformed mindset to manifesting the things you want . . . including the big things.

Here's an example from my life to show why commitment and immersion is so important. In the seventh grade, I took a beginning class in a foreign language: Spanish 101. And I did well enough in the class but had no interest in taking more advanced courses. However, I decided to take it again when I got to high school because I wanted an easy 'A' on my high school transcript. Then I took it yet again in college because I needed to fill in some required credits and I didn't want to work hard to do it. I was a lazy kid then, I know.

But I recall my college Spanish teacher (who was smoking hot, so I paid attention in class) recommending that in order to really learn Spanish we should come to the teacher's lounge where the Spanish teachers hang out, and immerse ourselves in the language. That way, she explained, would be the only way we would absorb the language and actually speak and understand it intelligently.

Well, I never did go to the teacher's lounge and I never got far beyond: "¿Cómo está usted?" So, practical knowledge of Spanish never became a part of me. And I regret that.

Many people approach manifesting the way I approached Spanish. That may explain why they never get very far with manifestation. They learn and practice a few affirmations or techniques from books or seminars. They might even experience some initial success because their enthusiasm is so high. However, they run into problems when the techniques eventually fail. When that happens they get discouraged and think, "Maybe manifestation is a bunch of New Age nonsense after all."

The problem is that those people never learn to think like true manifestors.

They scratch the surface, want fast success and hope to always get an easy 'A'. Unless they take the time to obtain the manifestation mindset, they will remain nothing more than dabblers and their results will forever reflect it.

For example, do you honestly think that people who use manifestation to win the lottery are dabblers? Do you believe they manifested their wins after trying out some technique once or twice or repeating "Millions of dollars flow to me" affirmations a dozen times? No! Most of those lottery winners have been working with lottery manifestation for a very long time, and the conditions were finally just right for a big win.

I know you don't want to be just a dabbler. If you intend to reliably use your ability to manifest wonderful things for the rest of your life, please absorb the nine manifestation strategies in the coming chapters for the next few weeks and make it a real part of you. Commit to this, and watch your abundance swell.

And now, onto the strategies!

MINDSET STRATEGY 1: APPRECIATE YOUR MANIFESTATION POWER

Did you know that your power to manifest favorable circumstances is active and flourishing right now? When you can positively say "yes" to that question, you are on your way to having the correct manifestation mindset and enjoying the abundance of life.

No matter what you think is missing, whether it's a mountain of money, world-wide fame, stellar accomplishments, a soul mate, more free time and luxuries, a career on the fast-track or ideal health, you have already successfully manifested countless true marvels. However, maybe you have not given yourself the credit for manifesting them—and it's vital that you do!

One of the best and easiest ways to develop your manifestation mindset is to get in the daily habit of recognizing and appreciating the wonderful things you already manifest every day. I know it sounds trite and simple, but all of the successful manifestors I talked with expressed appreciation for the many things they had manifested, and they consider that expression central to their success.

I recently read an article based on the works of Susan Jeffers, the author of **Feel the Fear and Do It Anyway**. If you haven't read that wonderful book, do yourself a favor and do it soon. The article stressed the importance of finding happiness in the *small activities* in life, rather than just the "grand splashes of brilliance," as Jeffers put it.

Speaking of gratitude, you may have heard that being grateful can help you manifest good things. That's because when you feel grateful, your mind and body emit a vibration to attract other people and circumstances that *correspond* with gratitude. For instance, wouldn't you like to attract people who are happy and grateful? Wouldn't you like to repel those people who are negative and nasty? I have a feeling you would.

But although many teachers and books insist on the importance of gratitude, they often neglect to tell you how to cultivate it. For example, if your marriage is in shambles and the rent is overdue, how are you supposed to feel grateful to the Universe when you feel only anger, resentment and fear? How many of us can quickly shift from fear to genuine gratitude during those difficult times? It's impossible to trick yourself into feeling grateful. Emotions cannot be faked.

Build a Gratitude Bridge

Fortunately, I found an easy way to take you from feelings of dissatisfaction to gratitude. I use it all the time to shift from one emotional state to another. I call it building a *gratitude bridge*.

It starts with an acceptance of your current circumstances. What's manifesting now is the result of what you thought, felt and did in the past. So, if your marriage is in trouble, you acknowledge that you have manifested that. If your boss is a tyrant and you hate your job, you accept that you attracted that situation.

Then, you acknowledge your feelings. If you are angry and frustrated, admit you feel that way.

Stop resisting what you have manifested, and accept that somehow you attracted your circumstances. Once you can do that, you will recognize that you also have the power to change them.

Next, spend a few minutes to think about the things that are going right for you. Don't tell me "nothing is going right," because you know that's not true. You can begin right where you are this very moment, and then widen your circle. For instance, you manifested this book. That seems like no big deal until you consider it carefully. You have manifested the time and funds to read this book. Think about the complexity involved to make such a "simple" thing happen. You are able to read and think and gain insight from these words. Your consciousness somehow engineered it, and that's impressive.

Now think about the healthy aspects of your body. Even if you have health challenges, there are undoubtedly aspects of your body and health that are still good. Accept the good you have manifested.

Did you eat within the last few hours? Did you sleep with a roof over your head last night? You manifested your food and shelter. Compared to a lot of people in the world, that makes you wealthy. Do you have a job that pays you enough to survive or some other means to support yourself? Acknowledge that you manifested those things. How many possessions do you own, and what are they? Acknowledge that. Can you think of any people you love and who love you? You attracted that love, and that's definitely something to fill you with gladness.

Chances are you took for granted all the amazing things you are responsible for manifesting. When you recognize how many things you have attracted that contribute to your well-being, you will discover you have manifested abundantly.

As you consider these manifestations, you are likely to experience positive emotions. For instance, you may feel *pleased* about them. You may be *proud* of attracting them. And like steps on a bridge, these emotions will lead to feelings of gratitude which seemed previously out of reach. These emotions allow you to move from one state of thinking to another.

When you decide to take delight in the *little things* you manifest in your daily life, true gratitude becomes easy to access.

Gratitude does not have to be sentimental. It can be a quiet joy. It can express itself as a happy recognition of your power to manifest during both negative and positive times. Once established as a part of your mindset, gratitude will contribute to your ability to manifest good things.

Reinforce Your Gratitude Bridge Daily

Here are the steps to construct and maintain your gratitude bridge:

1. As you go about your day, mentally identify at least five beneficial people, objects or circumstances in your life.

2. Silently appreciate that you manifested them.

3. Perform steps #1 and #2 every day, making the things you identify different each day. If you think about it, you have manifested so many good things you will never run out of options.

There is no need to choose extravagant things. For example, yesterday my five beneficial things were a cup of coffee, a hot shower, my reasonably full head of hair, a phone conversation with my elderly mother, an unexpected refund check that arrived in the mail. Today my five things included my three new pet finches, the tuna fish sandwich I had for lunch, ample time to do some work on this book, a creative idea that came to me as I wrote, and my good eyesight.

When you have performed this exercise daily for three weeks, appreciation will become a positive habit. Your gratitude bridge will be sturdy. You will start to appreciate every good thing you encounter, knowing you have manifested it. That's when you will know it has become part of your manifestation mindset.

Your mind will then vibrate gratitude throughout your day, and you will automatically attract good things.

MINDSET STRATEGY 2: INCREASE AND REINFORCE YOUR KNOWLEDGE

At this very moment, you are engaged in an outstanding way to develop a manifestation mindset: you are reading about it. The more you read about manifestation and the principles behind it, the more you will develop your mindset. Let me tell you why.

Have you ever noticed that the written word tends to carry more authority than the spoken word? For some reason it seems more important and worthy of your contemplation.

For example, here you are reading words written by someone you probably haven't met. Still, you are open to what these words convey about the nature of manifestation. Such is the power of the written word.

You form mental impressions based on what you read, abstract or realistic. The words and mental images create real memories, and your brain forges new connections. If what you are reading is interesting enough, these memories can have a tremendous influence on your thinking.

Therefore, when you read books, articles or even blog posts about manifestation and the Law of Attraction, you *literally affect your brain*. When you learn about a principle or technique that's new to you, your mind forms new associations. When you read familiar concepts, you strengthen pre-existing ones.

I have discovered that whenever I read about manifestation, it automatically stimulates my abilities. Why is this? I believe it's because the books affirm the power of manifestation which greatly influences the subconscious mind—which leads to real change.

What to Read

Obviously, it is up to you to decide which manifestation books to read. Thanks to the internet, there are lots of affordably-priced books of all kinds, even good free eBooks.

Read whatever appeals to you from a variety of authors. Some books, like the ones in this series, emphasize practical manifestation techniques. Others focus on one or two topics. Some are filled with inspiring stories. Some are classics, dating back through the corridors of time; others are newly published from some insightful authors. Some are for beginners; others are for advanced manifestation students.

For example, I have been working with manifestation for decades and only recently read Rhonda Byrne's *The Secret*. It's the book that popularized the Law of Attraction. I avoided it for many years because it seemed too commercial and elementary so I figured it contained nothing I didn't already know.

To make sure I wasn't unintentionally repeating its content, I finally decided to read it before the release of my first book in this series, *The Manifestation Manifesto*. To my surprise, I really enjoyed *The Secret*. It deserves its popularity, and is suitable for beginners and even advanced students and practitioners.

After you have read several books on manifestation, you will discover they share similar concepts and techniques. Don't let this dissuade you from continuing to read them. Yes, there is going to be overlapping information because the core principles remain the same.

But remember, reviewing manifestation principles reinforces the concepts in your brain and helps to create the right mindset. And I have found it helpful to read the same ideas reworded from different authors' perspectives.

Also, don't limit yourself to works that focus only on manifestation or the Law of Attraction. You may find books on related topics such as mindpower, thought vibration and metaphysical principles which can help you expand your knowledge and understanding.

If you have no idea what to read and where to start, here's a short list of books I've found helpful:

* *The Power of Your Subconscious Mind* by Joseph Murphy. Everyone should have a basic understanding of the subconscious because it is largely responsible for all that we manifest.

* *The Magic of Believing* by Claude Bristol. Filled with good stories and information about how belief triggers manifestation.

* *The Neville Reader* by Neville Goddard. A reader-friendly classic with ideas which continue to influence modern-day manifestation gurus.

* *The Field* by Lynne McTaggart. Offers a unique approach to the discussion of consciousness. An important work.

* *E3* by Pam Grout. A popular book with lots of experiments to verify the power of consciousness and manifestation.

* *The New Psycho-Cybernetics* by Maxwell Maltz. Updated from the classic book, it contains information about this subject with practical experiments to show what your inner mind can do.

* *The Kybalion* by Three Initiates. A must-have work on Hermetic principles relating to manifestation. Provides a strong foundation to understand this subject.

* *The Secret Science Behind Miracles* by Max Freedom Long. Discusses Huna (Hawaiian metaphysics) and offers ways to create rapport with the subconscious and the Higher Self.

* *Hawaiian Magic* by Clark Wilkerson. An obscure, profound book and one of my favorites. It's packed with unusual information and

unparalleled techniques to harness the power of the mind and body. Probably unlike anything you've ever read. Get it while you can!

* *The Holographic Universe* by Michael Talbot. Offers fascinating insights about the relationship between the mind and the universe. It will make you think and expand your perspective.

How to Read for Maximum Impact

While there may be no wrong way to read manifestation books, there are ways to optimize your reading style to more quickly create and fortify your manifestation mindset:

* *Read shortly before bedtime.* The best time to read material on manifestation is shortly before you go to sleep. Even though you will put the book aside for the night, your inner mind will continue to process the information.

* *Highlight passages.* There will be sentences or paragraphs in manifestation books which resonate with you. You may feel a sense that you were meant to read the book just for that important passage. So use the highlighting function on your reading device or write down the sections that speak to you. Even if you never read the passages again, the act of highlighting or writing them down more deeply reinforces a powerful impression.

* *Read frequently.* The goal is to regularly saturate your mind with affirming thoughts about

manifestation. Therefore, read for 15 minutes or so every day. It's okay if you skip a day, now and then. You don't want it to feel burdensome to you. But it is more effective to read a little bit more often, than it is to just sporadically binge-read.

MINDSET STRATEGY 3: STIMULATE YOUR CREATIVE, INTUITIVE MIND

Do you enjoy movies about time-travel, sci-fi, fantasy or superhuman abilities? If so, it may delight you to know that watching those genres of movies develops your manifestation mindset and may initiate some remarkable manifestations.

They reach and stimulate the creative, non-linear part of your mind. Ursula LeGuin, a superb writer of sci-fi and fantasy, in her excellent book **Language of the Night** explained how these kinds of genres bypass the part of the resistant, critical adult mind to deeply affect the subconscious or childlike part of the mind. LeGuin explained that when you remove that adult "critic" you can achieve more insight.

Here's an example. Think of how often toddlers do not judge what they do. They just go with it. How often have you seen a toddler try to stand up and walk and no matter how often she falls get right back up and try again – without judgment? Often adults just give up because we don't want to embarrass ourselves. We have to learn from the toddlers not to quit. They don't have the burden of the adult "critic".

Not only do those genres encourage a different kind of thinking and feeling, but they increase remarkable coincidences known as *synchronicities* and other unusual experiences. Let me share something with you to highlight how a movie can make an unexpected impact.

Recently I watched the sci-fi movie *Interstellar*. A trusted friend told me it was profound, and recommended it. Honestly, the night I watched it I thought the movie was okay and nothing to get particularly excited about. So I went to bed without giving it further thought.

However, the next day I was amazed by the memory of what I can only describe as a "meta-worldly" dream. Except it wasn't just a dream. Here is what I entered in my journal about it:

April 4, 2015

Last night I watched the movie Interstellar, and may have triggered some current 4th dimensional experience and memory.

Very hard to describe. I am "remembering" another reality concurrent with this one. It's as REAL as this one though. Having trouble remembering specifics, but I know it is relevant to this life and reality.

There are problems here I may be trying to resolve there. But when do I remember being there? The whole thing is freaky.

Details are on the edge of my memory. There are other people involved—I knew them, but can't place anyone or anything.

As you can imagine, that experience gave me a glimpse behind the scenes of the outer world we call "reality". There was a scene in the *Interstellar* movie which directly connected this to the part of my mind that might have been dormant.

And what makes it even more noteworthy is that I didn't consciously think too much about the movie as I watched it.

When my inner mind processed the ideas and images, the result was a life-changing experience that shifted my awareness and thinking. I will never forget that experience. And I owe it all simply to watching a sci-fi movie.

I am not suggesting you will have the same experience if you watch *Interstellar* or that anyone should watch any movies with that expectation. My experience merely illustrates the potential impact entertainment art can have on consciousness and mindset.

There are other movies that impacted my consciousness in less startling ways, but have been more important toward my overall mindset. For example, I own the *Groundhog Day* DVD, and I have watched it at least once a year on February 2nd since the year 2000. In case you haven't seen it, the movie is about a cynical, selfish man who relives the same day over and over until he redeems himself through genuine love and service.

Aside from being funny and entertaining, the movie is filled with messages about manifestation. The non-linear, creative time twist leaves a strong impression too. For example, a couple of years ago I noticed how I manifested the same problem-patterns with certain friendships. I recall thinking, "It's like Groundhog Day." Just like the character Phil, I knew I had the opportunity to make different choices in my thoughts and actions so I could break the recurring patterns and start to manifest healthier interpersonal relationships. The movie helped me recognize my own recurring pattern, and to change it.

There are many other movies which have contributed to my mindset with subtler, long-lasting effects. However, the goal with this strategy is not to recognize only profound revelations. It's to gently communicate and persuade the inner mind of the power of manifestation, and your ability to affect it.

What to Watch and How

Movies in the science fiction and fantasy genres are more likely to contribute to your developing manifestation mindset than others. They force you to suspend your disbelief and bypass the rational part of your mind.

Science fiction is often about considering new possibilities, expanding perspectives, reaching for things that appear beyond belief, and sometimes warning us of dire consequences.

Fantasy speaks in the language of the subconscious through metaphor and *archetypes*. We want to use the subconscious to fulfill our conscious desires. We want to use fantasy movies to connect with our deepest hopes and fears which we usually ignore or downplay or forget.

It's not about watching these kinds of movies for entertainment. The goal is to allow them to trigger a deeper awareness of your own manifestation powers.

With that in mind, here is a small collection of sci-fi/fantasy movies I have found to be very impactful (some are highly-reviewed). They are in no particular order: *The Matrix, Interstellar, Mr. Nobody, Lucy, Men in Black 3, Lord of the Rings, Dark City, Harry Potter: The Prisoner of Azkaban, Powder, Groundhog Day, X-Men: Days of Future Past, Star Wars, Star Trek, Edge of Tomorrow, Inception, Back to the Future, Sliding Doors, Limitless.*

When you see a movie you especially enjoy or that triggers something in you, please don't just watch it one time. Watch it again and again. The repetition will compound the effect of the messages. I recommend watching films of this type three times a week for at least the next 21 days.

MINDSET STRATEGY 4: CONDUCT MANIFESTATION EXPERIMENTS

Blindly believing in manifestation is a poor substitute for experience. To develop a strong mindset, you must have first-hand experience. By experimenting, you can test the manifestation principle and observe its power at work.

A coaching client recently asked me how often I actually work with manifestation techniques. I quickly replied, "Almost all of the time." It's true! I frequently run mini-manifestation experiments to search for patterns in my successes and failures, and then to deduce the cause-effect mechanisms. Those observations often lead to insights I can apply toward manifesting more important things.

People are usually attracted to manifestation initially because they hope to attract big things like millions of dollars or a perfect soul mate. There's nothing wrong with that. However, is your confidence strong enough to manifest those huge goals? Wouldn't it be easier to grow your manifesting confidence first?

By the way, the benefits of doing experiments like these goes way beyond mere confidence building.

Running frequent manifestation experiments trains your mind to search for the cause-effect relationship between your thoughts and outer circumstances.

It teaches you to recognize how past actions, thoughts and emotions affect your current circumstances. You discover how certain thinking patterns lead to positive or negative manifestations. You learn how to adjust your thoughts to create the best outcomes. And we'll discuss all of these more in a later strategy.

Five Mini-Manifestation Experiments

Here are five mini-manifestation experiments I have used with fantastic results. Some of them you can do right away to determine your results quickly. Other experiments take a few days to complete. I suggest you run at least two experiments per week for the next three weeks.

Not all experiments may succeed exactly the way you hope, but the goal here is to confirm your power to affect your reality.

Also, when you first succeed with some of these experiments your old mindset may question what caused those successes. You might simply decide the successes came from *selective attention* or even from luck. And you shouldn't be surprised about that.

But when you conduct the experiments often and then experience repeated successes, you will be convinced that your own mind and manifestation power are responsible for the outcomes. Any other explanations will seem extremely unlikely. Then, you will be on your way to your new mindset and be ready to go after bigger things.

Experiment #1: Manifest a compliment. The goal of this experiment is to manifest an unsolicited compliment from someone at the gym, at the workplace or any other environment you commonly visit. This experiment must be performed before you go to that venue. Here's how:

1. Sit down with a pen and a lined notepad (or use your tablet or computer).

2. Set a timer for five minutes.

3. Write a single statement to describe what you want to manifest. For example, "Someone will give me an uplifting compliment at the gym today." You do not need to be specific about the compliment. There's no need to worry about which person should give you the compliment either.

4. Start the timer, and write the manifestation statement over and over until the time is up.

5. Go on with your day, and see what happens.

I have often used the gym to run this experiment many times because it's convenient. My success rate has been excellent, and the results have sometimes been humorous. For instance, sometimes I've had someone give me a flirtatious glance or downright stare (a non-verbal compliment). Once I had a gym employee compliment me on being courteous for wiping down the equipment after I used it. Another time, a gym regular complimented me on looking stronger and leaner recently after I started a new diet-fitness plan.

Experiment #2: Manifest a song. Have you ever randomly started humming a song, and heard it on the radio a short time later? Did you think it was a coincidence? Maybe it was or wasn't. In this experiment, you *intentionally* manifest a song you haven't heard in a long time. It should not be something currently rising on the Billboard charts because that would be too easy to dismiss as coincidental. Instead, the song should be at least one year old and popular. Here's how to conduct the experiment:

* Choose a song to manifest. Ideally, it should be a song you know fairly well.

* Bring it to your mind, and sing it out loud frequently throughout the day.

* Affirm the intention that you want to hear the actual song.

* Do this every day until that song manifests.

It can be amusing to encounter how the song will manifest. For example, I recently ran this experiment and chose the song: "What Goes Around Comes Around" by Justin Timberlake. Anyway, I was in my car at a red light, cracked the window to free a trapped insect, and I noticed that very Timberlake song was blaring out of the car next to mine!

Other times, I've run this experiment and have heard the song manifested in various ways: while sitting in the dentist's office, at the grocery store, at the shopping mall, and even on a television commercial. It's often surprising when and where a song might show up.

Experiment #3: Coin Toss. Have you ever flipped a coin and guessed which side of the coin would show? You probably thought your chances were 50/50. In this experiment, you use your thought-power to manifest which side of the coin appears: heads or tails. You can run this several times in succession and see if you can beat the law of averages. Often you can! Remember, you are not trying to guess or predict the coin toss. You use your power of intention to *will* which side of the coin turns up. Here's how to conduct this experiment:

* Acquire a money coin.

* Determine which side you intend to manifest before the toss. You can use just your intention, or you can visualize or vocalize the result.

* Flip the coin, and observe the result.

* Repeat the procedure an even number of times, and record how many times you successfully manifested.

This is one of the fastest and simplest experiments to run. Sometimes I have run this experiment with spectacular results. More than once I have manifested "tails" ten out of ten tosses. Of course, there have been other times when my success rate was poor.

When you conduct this experiment often, you may find (as I have) that you generally manifest better and better over time. This is because your mindset has changed: whereas you once believed the coin toss was a matter of chance, you eventually come to realize that you influence it with your thoughts and emotions. Once the new mindset takes hold, you are more likely to get consistently good results.

When you get poor or lackluster results, it is not because manifestation is not working. There are many subtle factors that can have a bearing on your success rate. With careful observation, you will be able to determine what thoughts, feelings or conditions may be responsible for the results you achieve. Are you trying too hard? Does visualization help or hinder you? Are you tense or relaxed? Is someone watching as you experiment, and therefore affecting the outcome? All these things can be helpful to take into account.

You may also run this experiment with the roll of a die. You can have the intention of an odd or even choice, or you can manifest a particular number. For instance, use your power to manifest 6 on the die.

You may also perform this with a deck of playing cards to manifest a particular suit or even a specific card.

Experiment #4: Manifest a quarter. Have you experienced finding a shiny penny on the sidewalk? For this experiment, you use thought-power to manifest a quarter (or any coin you wish, wherever you live). The reason for using a quarter is because it's less common to find compared to a penny.

To work the experiment, vividly imagine and visualize that you find a quarter in a public place. Expect to find the quarter whenever you go for a walk. Do this frequently every day, and see how long it takes to manifest it.

I have conducted this experiment many times. Sometimes I do it from the premise of selective attention—that is, just by looking for them I'm likely to find them because there are many lost quarters. Other times, I choose to believe that by using the power of Mind and Thought I attract the quarter to me. I'll let you come to your own conclusion when you do the experiment.

Experiment #5: Manifest a message to yourself. In this intriguing experiment, you contemplate a question about some challenge you have that could be answered in just a few words. Then you expect an answer to appear in some form from the outer world. The message could show up on a stranger's t-shirt, a personalized license plate, a billboard, or in another way that interests you.

Here's an example. A manifestation/dream-coaching client of mine who now lives in India is excellent at manifesting specific messages to himself from words on strangers' t-shirts. He emails me often about these amazing synchronicities. Here's an (unedited) excerpt from one of his emails:

> *..on my way to the tea shop..(very close to a Shopping center which is close to where I happened to stay very*

close to .. 'Ispahani Center')..i was contemplating what to do with my new found 'free time'and then the of the top of my head were ideas about applying the 'Sankalpa Siddhi' techniques ..one of them being ....

.. 'Writing down intentions/goals/manifestations on Yellow Paper with Red Ink'...

..so I said to myself ok...I can do that..makes sense since I have more than enough time (I didn't really get down to doing it as I planned)..but I must have walked around half a minute and was adjacent to the wall of the 'Ispahani shopping center', when I noticed a guy (seemed like a student doing a course in an institute close by) who had on his T-SHIRT ...in UPPER CASE the words ..WRITE YOUR FUTURE.'

By the by today (20th Feb-Wednesday..Indian time) ... on the way back after buying a grilled chicken I happened to see the same T-SHIRT(and maybe the same guy)..

..at the Bus Stop right outside Ispahani center..

Here's how to run your own similar experiment:

1. Decide on a challenge you have in your life, or something you would like to confirm. If you can't think of anything, you can ask the Universe to send you a direct message of love or encouragement.

2. Concentrate on the question or topic for several minutes. Think about how wonderful it would be to receive some feedback from the Universe.

3. Go about your day, paying attention to the words and phrases that catch your eye.

4. Repeat the procedure every day—until you get your answer.

Note: This *does not* mean I'm saying you should take life-altering advice based on a message on a t-shirt or license plate. Please be reasonable and use discretion when you decide the manifested answer suggests a wise course of action.

MINDSET STRATEGY 5:
TRACK YOUR MANIFESTATIONS

Do you like to journal? Though it's not my favorite activity, I do it anyway because I discovered in the last year just how powerful writing down your thoughts can be and why tracking your manifestations must be included as a mindset strategy. Let me explain.

My ability to manifest has accelerated over the last year, and it took some introspection to find out why. What had I been thinking or doing over the last year to account for this sudden boost? Was it something I read or watched? Perhaps a new positive habit? When I finally deduced the reason, I laughed and said, "Aha!" I found that writing this series of books has greatly stimulated my manifestation power.

It was about a year ago when I began to work on my first manifestation book, *The Manifestation Manifesto*. A few months later I began to work on *The Manifestation Matrix*. Then I worked on this book. Hours of research, contemplation and analysis have been devoted to focusing on the principles, techniques and strategies of manifestation. During all of this, I noticed how quickly and effortlessly I manifested many desires and intentions. I thought about an old friend I hadn't see in decades and "Presto!" he contacted me within days. I thought about taking a trip to Los Angeles for a metaphysical conference and "Voila!" a way presented itself to do that at almost no cost. These are just two examples of many.

> **Writing down my ideas about the Law of Attraction and manifestation heightened my ability to manifest. I accidentally reinforced a manifestation mindset by the act of writing about it.**

However, you don't need to write books about manifestation to take advantage of this strategy. Instead, I suggest you keep a journal of your manifestation plans and adventures, and track your results from each manifestation experiment.

When you write down what you think, you are forced to slow down and organize yourself. When you are writing your thoughts, it might feel similar to putting pieces of a jigsaw puzzle together. Until you experience the benefits of journaling your thoughts though, you might not be able to see the whole picture or even how it might fit together. There might even be parts of the picture that make little sense until you see them from a distance.

When you develop the manifestation mindset suggested in this book, interesting things start to happen. You might become more creative, or make new connections between your thoughts, or experience dreams with symbolic meanings. You might have periods of doubt or buried emotions that start to come to the surface. Any of these can and should be written down in your journal.

Writing accentuates their relevance to you. Writing helps you cement your manifestation mindset. Recording your experiences in a journal or on your smartphone allows you to observe and monitor any improvements that may otherwise have gone unnoticed.

Write down any thought or activity related to what you want. Express what happened or what you want to happen. List any techniques you performed, any unusual coincidences, any messages from the Universe, any doubts.

Here are two recent, informal entries from my manifestation journal:

May 11, 2015. I had my recurring dream last night about attending classes at some big complex. Perhaps I am trying to learn or process something, but what? At the end of the dream, it seems I am always packed up and ready to go home. Could "home" represent the material plane of manifestation?

I received an unexpected check in the mail today from some class action lawsuit regarding some food supplement I guess I bought years ago. The check amount wasn't much, but it's a nice surprise.

I found two quarters today which is funny because I have just included that experiment in the future Mindset book. How's that for synchronicity!?

***

May 12, 2015. While driving home from Joe's house, I turned on my usual radio news station. However, instead of news, they were playing an infomercial about the food supplement creatine. This is remarkable because I have been considering the possible benefits of creatine for Mom because I've learned that it can be very beneficial for seniors to retain muscle and improve brain function. The infomercial explained the brain aspect very well. It was useful information. I'm going to clear it with her doctor first, and then suggest she give it a try.

The Manifestation Matrix *reached #1 in two categories! Now that I've manifested that, perhaps it's time to reach higher.*

Started watching Mr. Nobody movie at Lisa's recommendation. Not what I expected, and a little slow for my taste but I'll finish it and see how it impacts me.

Journaling Alternatives

There are all kinds of ways to journal. One of my clients keeps a type of journal in the form of emails he writes to me. When something remarkable or even noteworthy occurs, he emails me about it. He finds it more enjoyable than a traditional journal because he knows someone is reading it and may respond, rather than writing only for self-reflection. Truthfully, I don't always have the time or opportunity to respond to everything he emails about because he writes long and often. But I don't discourage his emails because I know they help him to chronicle his experiences, and he's able to sort them out and make sense of his observations.

So if a traditional journal is not your thing, consider creating a folder of emails, writing a blog or joining a group on Facebook to process and share your experiences. Besides helping you, this could help people who will be inspired by your manifestation adventures.

MINDSET STRATEGY 6: PERFORM ACTIVE AND PASSIVE AFFIRMATIONS

Affirmations have been around a long time, and they often remain a standard recommendation of life coaches, self-help gurus and many psychologists. While I consider them insufficient as a stand-alone strategy for personal transformation, affirmations can and should be used to help create your new manifestation mindset.

Affirmations were first made popular in the 1920s by French psychologist Emile Coué. Coué's method centered on repeating twenty times a day the phrase, "Every day, in every way, I'm getting better and better." His idea was that over time the statements are accepted by the subconscious as true, and changes in thinking, attitude and behavior will follow.

Not only are affirmations effective for self-improvement, weight loss, and self-esteem building, they can be used to establish and reinforce the manifestation mindset. They also help to target specific areas of life where manifesting is most desirable, such as with acquiring money, love or health. Nearly all of the successful manifestors I interviewed have used affirmations in some form and credit it, in part, for their accomplishments. I use them too.

There are two kinds of affirmations: active and passive. Active affirmations are those you recite aloud. Passive affirmations are recited to you through recordings, for example.

Nine Affirmations to Develop Your Manifestation Mindset

You may imitate the above method by replacing Coué's mantra with statements that focus on manifestation.

Below are several affirmations. Select one and commit it to memory, then recite it throughout the day. For greater effectiveness, whenever possible, recite it out loud at least 21 times:

* "Day by day, I grow more aware of and confident with my manifestation abilities."

* "I use the power of Thought to positively shape my life and circumstances."

* "My mind draws the people, objects and situations I need to fulfill my desires."

* "I witness proof of my ability to create my reality."

* "The Universe favorably responds to my intentions, and manifests what I want."

* "I manifest ever increasing prosperity, loving relationships and good health."

* "My power to manifest abundance unfolds like a blooming flower."

* "As I develop my manifestation mindset, whatever I want comes to me quickly and automatically."

* "The quality of what I manifest depends on the thoughts I choose to dwell upon."

After you have worked with an affirmation for a day or more, you may switch to another one. You do not have to use every affirmation on the list, and you are welcome to compose your own.

However, make sure the affirmations you use are statements you consciously consider true and realistic. Otherwise, you may set up a conflict between your conscious mind and your subconscious. For example, affirmations like, "I instantly manifest a billion dollars" might be rejected if you believe the statement seems far-fetched or unattainable.

To make this technique passive, you may also make a recording of the affirmations and listen once or twice a day. To do so, slowly and clearly read and record each affirmation once. Also pause five seconds between each affirmation, because this will help your mind to absorb them better.

Affirmations through Music

Listening to songs that affirm your power to manifest provides a wonderful alternative way to apply affirmations. It's one of my favorite strategies.

About a week ago, I heard the 1989 Roy Orbison song "You Got It" on the radio. After that, it stuck in my head for the next several days. And I found myself at random times singing aloud, day and night: *"Anything you want, you got it. Anything you need, you got it. Anything at all, you got it, baby."* What a fantastic manifestation message to affirm!

Music, by its very nature, stimulates passions and emotions. When we hear or sing a lyric along with a melody, it evokes emotions and creates a strong impression on the inner mind. It communicates with both the rational and the creative parts of the mind. When we listen and sing with the same song over and over, as we often do with songs we enjoy, the effect is multiplied.

To use this method of affirmation delivery you must find and listen to songs that support manifestation power. In my example, the chorus is the only part of the song that truly fits this principle. This is acceptable as long as the rest of the lyrics are uplifting. There are songs with lyrics which from beginning to end affirm manifestation power, and those are ideal.

Here is a playlist of mine with song examples that apply to this principle:

Natasha Bedingfield: "Unwritten"

Jason Mraz: "Anything You Want"

Shakira: "Give It Up To Me"

Brand New Heavies: "You Are The Universe"

Des'ree: "You Gotta Be"

Olivia Newton John: "Magic"

Moody Blues: "The Voice"

America: "You Can Do Magic"

George Harrison: "Got My Mind Set On You"

I don't expect you to like the same kind of music I enjoy. I'm sharing my list so you can check out some of these songs to get an idea of lyrics which promote a manifestation mindset.

Your task is to collect songs that match your taste, put them on your phone, laptop/tablet or music device, and listen to them frequently for at least 21 days. And, whenever possible, sing along with them to maximize their impact.

Because of how music embeds itself in your consciousness and connects you with strong and subtle emotions, this method of affirmation delivery and absorption is unmatched. I recommend it.

MINDSET STRATEGY 7:
SELF-GUIDED MEDITATION FOR
MANIFESTORS

Most of the successful manifestors I've interviewed work with meditation in some way. They consider it to be an important part of their manifestation process. A large number of them use guided meditations where another person takes them into a relaxed state of consciousness. The meditations are often accompanied by imagery, affirmations or suggestions designed to create an impression on the inner mind.

When you are relaxed, the critical part of your mind is quieted. In daily life, this censor is good because it keeps you from acting on everything people ask or tell you to do. For example, can you imagine what would happen if you acted on every sensational advertisement?

However, when it comes to embracing a new mindset this censor can work *against* you. For instance, suppose you have a long-term belief that world resources are scarce and it's a "dog eat dog world." But you wish to believe "there is an abundant supply of resources, and love is the core nature of humanity." This would create a problem because the critical part of your mind would sense the clash between the new and old ideas. It often rejects the new.

It is not enough to want to believe an idea or principle. Your subconscious mind must truly accept it, or your mindset will not change.

Guided meditation offers an efficient way to *convince* your subconscious of the reality of your manifestation power. It also does not require nearly as much repetition as traditional affirmations because it bypasses resistance through the slowing of your brainwaves that takes place during meditation.

Below is what is known as a *self-guided meditation*, where you narrate the meditation. You don't need to close your eyes, and you don't need to record it and play it back. Instead, you just read the words as instructed and it will automatically guide you into the right state. Virtually anyone with a good grasp of the English language can do it.

In the mid-1990s, I discovered it's easy to produce a relaxed, meditative state while you read aloud. It was so effective for me and my clients and students that in 2004 I published my first bestselling book about it. If you would like to understand more about how it works, please see the list of my published books in the **Books+ chapter** at the end of this book. I promise it will be worthwhile, and it will help you achieve your manifestation goals.

Now let me get into how you use the self-guided meditation to communicate messages of empowerment to your inner mind. Remember, creative imagery invokes your imagination and gets your mind to think in an effective and concentrated way about manifestation. I call this self-guided meditation the Manifestation Powerhouse Meditation. And you will understand why as you read it.

Use it twice a week for at least three weeks to help establish and strengthen your new mindset. You can start to use it right now if you have a few minutes.

Reading Instructions

* Sit in a comfortable chair, where you won't be disturbed for 10 to 15 minutes.

* Read the Manifestation Powerhouse Meditation aloud using a calming tone of voice (you can do it silently as well, if you are concerned about disturbing anyone).

* During the meditation, notice how the words in parentheses are directions meant for you to follow. You don't read those aloud.

* When you see " . . . ", pause for a moment before continuing.

* When you are prompted to pause, make sure to obey.

* When you finish reading, clap your hands once or twice to ensure a return to everyday consciousness.

* Give yourself several minutes after this session to make sure you are stable and steady before you drive a vehicle, etc. This is important for

everyone's safety, of course. You could be so involved and sensitive you might need to be more careful.

"Manifestation Powerhouse Meditation"

"As I read this self-guided meditation out loud, I speak in a relaxed tone of voice . . . and by reading slower (read slower) . . . and even more s-l-o-w-l-y (read very slowly) . . . I realize how my voice completely calms me . . . and I feel content. (Pause five seconds.)

"This peaceful feeling reminds me of a care-free walk along the beach on a warm, sunny day. I imagine my feet upon the soft sand as I look and listen to the waves which break upon the shore. (Pause and imagine seeing and listening to waves.)

"As I stand on the shoreline . . . water and sea-foam washes over my feet (pause and imagine it).

"A breeze passes over my body, and I can smell the fresh, salty air of the sea (pause and imagine).

"I sit down on the sand, and the healing sunshine embraces my body like a warm, soothing blanket. I feel the glow on my face . . . and it descends onto my shoulders and my back . . . automatically loosening the muscles . . . in my arms . . . hands and fingers . . . bright golden yellow sunshine soothing my chest . . . warming and calming my torso . . . my legs . . . all the way down to my toes.

"My mind relaxes and effortlessly drifts . . . and like clouds in the sky, my thoughts take on interesting and beautiful shapes. They then change into other shapes. Drifting . . . moving . . . shifting . . . thoughts and images.

"And with the slightest intention, I can create images in my mind . . . even with my eyes open . . . as I read.

"As I count backwards from five to one, I relax deeper and deeper as I imagine each number.

"Right now, I form the number five in my imagination. (Pause and imagine it.)

"And I relax deeper . . . as I now form the number four in my mind. (Pause and imagine it.)

"More at ease with every number . . . as I next form the number three. (Pause and imagine it.)

"Ever deeper relaxed and at peace . . . I now imagine the number two . . . (Pause and imagine it.)

"The number one . . . (Pause and imagine it.)

"I am now in a deeply relaxed state of mind and body, and feel better than I have in a long time. I am open and receptive to positive ideas and images about my power to manifest. (Pause five seconds.)

"I am a manifestation powerhouse.

"My thoughts and feelings are invested with tremendous energy to change and create the world around me.

"Everything I say, do, think, feel and believe contributes to the Universe.

"Like throwing a stone into a pond, the energy of my mind sends ripples through the waters of time and space.

"Like a magnet, the force of my intention draws to me people, objects and situations. Some things come quickly. Others take longer. But everything responds to me in time. They do come. The thoughts I think and the words I say never return empty.

"I imagine I stand at the top of a tall hill where I see all around a large, green meadow with many blooming flowers. I pretend that my whole body grows larger and taller . . . until I am the size of a giant. Now I can see for hundreds of miles in every direction. In the distance I observe forests, mountains, valleys and rivers, small towns and great cities.

"As I stand straight and so tall and I close my eyes . . . I transform myself into a great radio tower. My body is the metal scaffolding of that tower, and it tapers up to a point where my head would be. And where the center of my forehead would be, just between the eyebrows, there is a bright, pulsing electric light. From this light I broadcast all my thoughts and intentions . . . with a vibrating signal that goes through the air . . . with great power and amplitude . . . in every direction.

"My thoughts are strong and vibrate throughout the land. I see waves of energy go forth from me. My signal reaches near and far . . . to all people, places or things that are in harmony with my thoughts, desires and intentions. They rally to my cause and respond to my intentions and desires. They become my agents and my allies and to achieve the most effective manifestation.

"The more I focus on any thought, the stronger the signal I broadcast to the Universe. Therefore, I dwell on thoughts of prosperity, love, happiness and good health. These manifest through the supportive people and the fortunate circumstances I attract.

"I now imagine myself as a human body again, back to my normal size. From now on, I think of myself as a manifestation powerhouse. I forevermore know my body and mind transmit my thoughts and desires to the Universe. And the Universe responds by manifesting all the things that bring me peace, joy and balance in every area of my life.

"Every time I read this self-guided meditation, I will relax deeper than the time before.

"I will now count up from one to five to end this meditation and return to regular consciousness.

"One . . . I begin to emerge from this self-guided meditation.

"Two . . . I am returning to my everyday state of wakefulness.

"Three . . . I feel my mind and body rousing moment by moment.

"Four . . . I am ready to emerge completely.

"Five . . . I am wide awake and ready to continue my day."

(end of meditation)

MINDSET STRATEGY 8:
WEAR A "MAGIC"
MANIFESTATION TALISMAN

Can you imagine how confident you would feel if you had a magic talisman to perpetually boost your manifestation ability? This extraordinary strategy I'm going to tell about will turn that into reality for you.

Select an article of jewelry (or clothing if you prefer) that represents manifestation to you, and wear it every day. It will subconsciously remind you every minute of the day that the Law of Attraction is at work and that you manifest your reality. In time, your inner mind will come to embrace manifestation as solidly true.

I first discovered this strategy by accident and passed it on to my self-help clients. One year for my birthday, my sister gave me a signet ring bearing the cross of the Knights Templar because she knew my fascination with their mystical legends. Whenever I put the ring on, it was a playful way to connect with the mythical power of the Knights Templar. I imagined that whenever I wore the ring, I had access to virtuous power, strength and nobility.

However, after I stopped pretending, I noticed whenever I wore the ring that I felt a shift in my attitude and behavior without consciously trying. I was more confident, even courageous and I carried myself with more dignity. It was as if the ring became magical.

What really happened is the ring became a symbolic reminder to my subconscious mind, and it activated the virtues the ring represents.

Ever since, I have used this concept as a technique to boost and develop manifestation power.

Here's one more example: I purchased another piece of jewelry with a spiral design on it that made me think of manifesting. My first metaphysical teacher taught me that the "spiral" symbolizes expanding consciousness and the whirling motion which is connected with all manifestation. When I wear the spiral, it automatically reinforces my mindset toward abundance and it magnetizes good fortune to me very often. It's like having someone every second of the day quietly whisper in my ear, "Your manifestation power is active and available."

This idea goes back to the ancients, because luck charms have been around for thousands of years and they work in a similar way. When someone *believes* in a luck charm and carries it around with them, the charm serves as a constant affirmation that good luck will manifest—and so it does.

It works like a placebo. Placebos are pills with no medicinal value, but work for a large number of those people who take them because they believe they will work. Likewise, if someone believes finding a four-leaf clover will bring them luck, that person's mind will attract lucky circumstances. The power is not in the four-leaf clover, it's in the powerful energy of the mind.

It's Not Magic, It's Energy

However, I propose that there is more to a magic talisman than the placebo effect. Something peculiar happens to an object when it is worn regularly with a specific intention:

The object retains the energy of what is intended, and independently radiates that intention to the Universe.

Think about it, and it will make sense. Because everything is made of thought-energy, including rings and necklaces, whenever you wear a piece of jewelry, some of your thought-energy or thought-essence transfers to that piece of jewelry. That's why clairvoyants sometimes use a piece of jewelry to connect with the energy of its owner. The jewelry absorbs the energy of its wearer. The longer and more frequently someone wears an item, the more energy it transfers. When the item has a special purpose or intention behind it, the item becomes imbued with the thought-energy of that intention.

So once you have worn your manifestation talisman for many days, it absorbs more of the energy connected with your intention. Charged with thought-energy, it then radiates that intention 24 hours a day, whether you are aware of it or not. In a sense, it really does become a magic talisman!

If that disturbs you because of your life philosophy, then don't think of it as magic. Think of it as transferred thought-energy. It will work just the same.

What Kind of Talisman to Choose

Your talisman doesn't have to be a ring. You may choose any jewelry you prefer, as long as it's something you can wear virtually all day. It's up to you whether it's something that will be visible to others or worn under your clothes.

The most obvious choices are to use a ring or a bracelet or a necklace. What it's made of, how much it costs and whether it is plain or displays a symbol are entirely your choice. Whatever it is, the item should remind you of manifestation in some way, and it needs to be assigned exclusively to that purpose. If it isn't special to you, then your subconscious won't think of it as special either and then it won't serve its purpose.

How to Use Your Manifestation Talisman

Once you have selected the item, it's easy to put it to work. Here are the steps:

1. Whenever you put the item on (e.g. in the morning as you dress for your day), take a moment to regard what it represents. No need to make a huge production of it. Just look at it and think or say something like, "This ring symbolizes that the Law of Attraction is always at work in my life, and I manifest prosperity and happiness."

72

2. For the next 30 seconds, imagine it giving you a boost of manifestation power and confidence.

3. Go about your day knowing its presence perpetually affirms your manifestation power.

4. Repeat steps 1-3 every day.

After you have performed this procedure for a number of consecutive days, the power of your talisman becomes automatic. And you no longer need to affirm its importance or imagine that it is boosting your power. You can just put it on, and it will work without any further effort or conscious input.

Also, it is unwise to tell other people about your talisman or lend it to them. If someone notices the item your wearing and asks you about it, don't mention manifestation to them. Their responses might negatively affect the way you think about this technique and your talisman. It's better to keep silent about it.

MINDSET STRATEGY 9:
BUILD POSITIVE EXPECTATION

This final strategy helps you create positive expectation, because when you genuinely expect to manifest your thoughts and desires you will have a highly developed manifestation mindset. In a way, you might say I've saved the best manifestation strategy for last because it is so easy and yet so extremely powerful.

I want to let you in on a little secret: I owe much of my success as a hypnotherapist to my ability to create expectation in my clients. When they fully expect to be safely and successfully hypnotized, it's easy to hypnotize them. When they leave my office after the session and expect to stop smoking, lose weight, be more confident, or make some other important change in their lives—then most often that's exactly what happens for them. The reason for this may seem obvious:

We tend to receive what we expect.

Happily, this tendency doesn't just apply to hypnosis and habit change. It also applies to manifesting. Positive expectation energetically and psychologically puts you in an excellent frame of mind for manifesting.

Expectation is an unmatched antidote for doubt because it inherently carries belief without the need for self-conscious effort. When you expect something to happen, your belief in it is understood. You calmly anticipate that whatever thoughts you focus on will unquestionably show up in your environment in some way. Any anxiety about potential failure is altogether avoided.

However, the benefits of positive expectation go even further because it contains a vital formula for manifestation:

Positive expectation causes you to naturally form recurring, stable images of what you expect. Unhindered by doubt and anxiety, those consistent and realistic mental images inevitably lead to manifestation.

For instance, when you expect to manifest a beach vacation—whether you are consciously aware of it or not—your inner mind pictures the kind of beach you love and the activities you expect to enjoy there. Your subconscious conjures sense-images of waves undulating onto the shore, or a series of walks on warm sand, or the welcome smells of the moist, salty air, of lounging in the warm sun while you sip a Mai Tai or an iced tea. Charged with the emotion of positive anticipation, these images act like magnets that seem to inevitably attract the circumstances necessary to manifest what you want in the material world.

How to Build Positive Expectation

As simple as the idea of positive expectation is, there is a catch. It must be absolutely authentic. It cannot be faked. For example, you cannot talk yourself into genuinely expecting to meet your soul mate. You either expect to meet her, or it's really just a wish or a hope tinged with doubt.

So how do you build positive expectation? How do you get to a point where you expect your thoughts to manifest? In an earlier strategy, you were given mini-experiments to test and observe your manifestation ability firsthand. This strategy takes that idea even further, and is in some ways the core of the manifestation mindset:

Learn to see the outer world as your own giant feedback system for your thoughts.

Make a daily habit of watching situations as they arise in your life. Search for meaning in everything that happens to you. When anything interesting occurs, whether big or small, good or bad, be aware that your thoughts, feelings and past actions manifested it. Ask yourself why and how it did. Here are some specific questions to ask:

* Is this event a manifestation of my thoughts?

* Did I intend to manifest this or is it unintentional?

* What thoughts and emotions might be responsible for attracting this situation?

* Have I manifested something similar before? Is this a pattern?

* What can I learn from this about my manifestation abilities?

After a while, you will find clear parallels between certain thoughts and what you manifest. You will gain insight into the intricate workings of your own mind, and how certain thought-habits lead to pleasant or unpleasant situations.

When you think in specific ways, you will expect to manifest certain kinds of things.

When that happens, you will have learned to create positive expectation. You may then choose to adjust your thoughts. For example, there came a point recently when I observed how my permissive kindness attracted people who took advantage of me. I figured if I didn't change my thoughts I would attract more of the same kinds of people. So I established stronger personal boundaries to develop greater self-respect. Once I did those things, I expected to manifest balanced relationships and to attract those who properly respected me. And that's exactly what's happened.

Many people wonder why it's difficult to quickly manifest a lot of money, instant fame or another grand overnight success. One reason is that no matter how many affirmations of "I manifest a million dollars" those people may recite, the truth is they really don't expect to receive it. Like I said, there's no faking it: You won't fool your subconscious.

Positive expectancy must be earned.

The way to do that is by working with manifestation on a daily basis until you know what you can expect.

Eventually, it is entirely conceivable that you will be able to expect amazing things to manifest quickly.

HOW TO KNOW WHEN YOU HAVE ACHIEVED THE MANIFESTATION MINDSET

After the 21-day period, how will you know for sure you have acquired the manifestation mindset?

When manifesting becomes an automatic part of your everyday thinking process, it's a strong indicator you have achieved the right mindset.

To give you an example from my own life, recently I thought about Cheers, the American sitcom from the 1980s. I had not watched it in years. I remembered a funny episode where a literary magazine rejects a poem Dianne submits and publishes Sam's.

I thought it might be nice to see that smart and witty episode again, but I didn't mention it to anyone nor did I think about it any longer. However, later the same day, I discovered a family member had recorded that same Cheers episode! This was remarkable because this family member never expressed an interest in the show.

As I sat down to watch it, I laughed not only at the jokes from the show but also at the way my thoughts had quickly and unexpectedly manifested that particular episode. This kind of thing happens to me frequently because of the manifestation mindset I've acquired.

When I told my friend Jeff about the Cheers synchronicity, he said it was just a coincidence. In High School, he and I were religious fundamentalists. When we phased out of that particular mindset we went our different ways, philosophically-speaking. I became metaphysically-oriented. Jeff became a rationalist, atheist and skeptic. He is sure that nothing exists beyond the physical dimension that we can see and touch. For him, the notion that our thoughts manifest reality is a silly fantasy and just magical thinking because "it doesn't hold up to the scientific method."

Of course, even before I asked him I knew what he would say about the Cheers incident. But I enjoy having my own perspective challenged, and it amuses me to hear him rationalize things that don't fit into his worldview.

Because of my mindset, I am aware that my mind manifested that Cheers episode. The cause and effect appear obvious: I thought about the episode with positive emotion, had a desire and intention to see it, and the conditions were right for the Universe to manifest it for me. I've had way too many experiences just like it to explain it any other way. The relationship between my thoughts and what shows up in my life is a given, and I see proof of it every single day.

Even though other people may offer
contrary viewpoints, when you recognize
that your thoughts are responsible for

manifesting things—then you have attained the manifestation mindset.

When you have used the nine manifestation strategies and you make sure the quote above applies, you may reduce how often you implement them. Keep this in mind too. For some people, 21 days may not be enough time to establish thought habits that comprise the manifestation mindset. The latest research indicates that it takes an average of 66 days to form a new habit pattern. As a clinical hypnotherapist and coach since 1997, I agree with that estimate. For some it's takes less time, for others more, but on average it takes 66 days. Therefore, if you are not sure whether you have acquired the manifestation mindset after using the strategies for 21 days I urge you to continue for at least another 45 days. Then, reevaluate whether the thought-shift has become a welcome habit.

In fact, the strategies are so easy to incorporate it's my hope you will continue with some or all of them indefinitely. For in truth, you never stop developing the manifestation mindset. You never stop learning, experimenting and expanding your awakening thought-power.

Your manifestation mindset is a growing, living thing, and it will serve you for the rest of this life . . . and beyond.

Happy manifesting!

BOOKS+

The Manifestation Manifesto: Amazing Technique and Strategies to Attract the Life You Want—No Visualization Required - This is the first book in Forbes Robbins Blair's Amazing Manifestation Strategies series. It's packed with over 20 manifestation techniques, emphasizing how to attract what you want and how to defeat negativity. See why this book became a bestseller.

The Manifestation Matrix: Nine Steps to Manifest Money, Success and Love When Asking and Believing Are Not Working - The second in the Amazing Manifestation Strategies series, this book provides an easy, powerful step-by-step formula to manifest whatever you want. It includes clear and practical steps which take only about an hour to complete, so you can put this manifestation system to work now.

Attract Surplus Money Mp3 - Based on a script from the book *More Instant Self Hypnosis*, this bestselling hypnotic audio Mp3 programs your mind to attract more money. Soothing and effective, you can download and listen to it instantly.

The Genie Within: Your Wish is Granted - Based on classes Mr. Blair taught in the Baltimore-Washington DC area, this ebook and Mp3 audio course teaches you how to acquire your own genie lamp so you can better use your imagination to manifest your wishes. It is innovative, effective, fun and easy to do.

Soul of the Knight: Awaken the Warrior Within - Tap into your inner confidence, discipline and motivation as you connect with the noble knight within. This ebook/audio Mp3 program is like nothing else out there. If you are drawn to the image of medieval Knights, this program can help you to transform your life quickly and dramatically. Mr. Blair believes it's the most powerful product he's ever produced. Download it now.

Instant Self Hypnosis: How to Hypnotize Yourself With Your Eyes Open - Stop smoking, lose weight, and stop stressing out. In his original bestselling book, Forbes Robbins Blair reveals his remarkable eyes-open self-hypnosis method that allows you to hypnotize yourself as you read. This bestselling classic book contains 35 powerful scripts to improve your life in practical ways. You'll use this book again and again.

More Instant Self Hypnosis: Hypnotize Yourself as You Read - The sequel to *Instant Self Hypnosis*, this book contains 48 self-improvement scripts covering a wide variety of topics such as "Achieve Your Potential" and "Feel More Sexy." Includes Master Induction 2.0, an improvement on the original script from his first book. There are also new interactive experiments to help you understand self hypnosis better while it prepares you to hypnotize yourself as you read. In other words, you only have to read to succeed.

Self Hypnosis As You Read: 42 Life Changing Scripts - "Lose the Last 10 Pounds," "Never Be Late Again," "Save More Money." These are a few of the hypnosis script titles in Forbes Robbins Blair's newest self-hypnosis book. Its script topics are the most requested by readers and fans of *Instant Self Hypnosis* and *More Instant Self Hypnosis*. These scripts induce hypnosis with the author's eyes-open self-hypnosis method. Includes advanced material never before released. Some readers say it is Mr. Blair's best self-hypnosis book.

Self Hypnosis Revolution: The Amazingly Simple Way to Use Self Hypnosis to Change Your Life - Learn how even mundane, daily tasks like taking out the garbage or brushing your teeth can be used to create remarkable transformations in five key areas of your life. This innovative autosuggestion method is easy, fun and effective. And, unlike other self hypnosis methods it requires no extra time from your day.

ABOUT THE AUTHOR

Forbes Robbins Blair is a long-time student and practitioner of all things metaphysical. This is the third book in his Amazing Manifestation Strategies series which include **The Manifestation Manifesto** and **The Manifestation Matrix**. He has taught metaphysics classes on the US east coast, and has been on national radio many times for his expertise in hypnosis, dream symbolism and manifestation.

He is a clinical hypnotherapist and the author of several self-hypnosis books, including the bestselling hypnosis book **Instant Self Hypnosis: How to Hypnotize Yourself with Your Eyes Open**.

Mr. Blair considers it a privilege to share what he knows with his readers.

Visit Forbes' website: <u>forbesrobbinsblair.com</u>

REQUEST

I appreciate you taking the time to read The Manifestation Mindset, and for allowing me to share my approaches with you.

If you enjoyed this book, please write a customer review. Your opinion really makes a difference.

Thanks,

Forbes

Made in the USA
Lexington, KY
12 May 2016